How to
Impress the Cognoscenti
and
Perplex the Hoi Polloi

A light-hearted compendium
of
foreign phrases used in English

By Ed Bliss

Cartoons by Tom Stiglich

ISBN: 145389411X
ISBN-13: 9781453894118

Printed by CreateSpace, An Amazon Company

This book is dedicated to
Libby,
whose idea it was

Introduction

Foreign words and phrases, used sparingly and appropriately, supplement the richness and variety of the English language, but millions of people wince when they see a strange phrase in italics, not knowing what it means or how it is pronounced. The pages that follow were written to help such people.

Of course, using foreign words and phrases incorrectly, or too frequently, is to be avoided. After all...

> Some folks misuse foreign terms,
> A practice they employ
> To impress the *cognoscenti*
> And perplex the *hoi polloi.*

In case you don't already know it, the Italian word *cognoscenti* means those having superior knowledge, and *hoi polloi* means everyone else. After reading these verses you will probably consider yourself clearly in the first category.

– EB

Sunning on some tropic isle,
   That's where I'd like to be.
No boss, no bills, no winter chills,
   That's living *sans souci*.

(sanh soo-SEE) Without worries or cares.

1

It's fun to go out sailing,
　　But you should be aware
An unintended consequence
　　Is sometimes *mal de mer.*

(mahl de mehr) Seasickness.

If the Queen of England asks you
　　To come to tea some day,
To reply, "I'm rather busy,"
　　Is a gross *lèse majesté.*

(lez mah-zhes-TAY) An affront to the sovereign.

My best friend has moved in with me,
　　But doesn't help with rent.
When I said, "*Mi casa, su casa,*"
　　That's not quite what I meant.

(*mee kaw-sa soo kaw-sa*) My house is your house.

When you're getting together a chamber group
　　To perform a fugue or sonata,
If a guy shows up with a saxophone
　　He is clearly *persona non grata.*

(per-SOH-nah non GRAH-tah) An unwelcome or
unacceptable person.

Their friendship is cordial but only platonic,
　　Or so the couple contends,
But when they were caught *in flagrante delicto*
　　It was clear they were more than just friends.

(in flah-GRAHN-tay de-LIK-toh) In sexual activity.

The concept of *noblesse oblige*
　　Means people in high stations
Acknowledge that their lofty state
　　Involves some obligations.

(no-BLESS o-BLEEGE) Nobility requires; the
understanding that privilege entails responsibilities.

The little dog was tethered by
　A jewel-encrusted leash.
It proved his owner had arrived
　Among the *nouveau riche*.

(*noo-voh-REESH*) Persons who have recently
become wealthy.

Though Van Gogh's early work was scorned,
  And met with jeers and taunts,
His paintings now are recognized
  As art *par excellence.*

(par ex-seh-LAHNS) Preeminent, superior.

Though several nations have a list
  Of colonies they've owned,
The idea of self-governance
  Is spreading *tout le monde.*

(too le MOHND) Throughout the world.

Some salesmen like to ply their trade
  With whiskey, gin, or brandy.
To weaken sales resistance,
  That's their *modus operandi.*

(mo-dus op-er-AND-ee) Method of operation.

The judging of a painting
   Provokes profound debate.
What I deem *ne plus ultra*
   You call second rate.

(nay ploos UL-trah) Perfection, that which
nothing is beyond, the acme.

The huckster approached a young woman
   With dozens of items to tempt her.
The jewelry she bought turned out to be hot.
   The lesson? *Caveat emptor!*

(KAH-vee-aht EMP-tor) Let the buyer beware.

Magna cum laude at graduation
   Looks nice beside your name.
Summa cum laude is better yet —
   The ultimate acclaim.

(MAG-nah koom LOW-day) With high honors.
(SUM-mah koom LOW-day) With highest honors.

To assist you with the housework
   And to help with children's care
In return for board and room, you might
   Consider an *au pair.*

(*oh PAIR*) A foreign young person providing help with
housework and child care in exchange for food and lodging.
The French term means equal exchange.

When faced with specious arguments
   (And everybody's heard 'em)
One way to turn the tables is
   Reductio ad absurdum.

(*ree-DUK-tee-oh ad ab-SUR-dum*) Proving the falsity of a
statement by showing its absurdity when followed to its
logical conclusion.

I love to be with wife and kids,
   I actually adore 'em,
But every man, at times, must have
   His own *sanctum sanctorum.*

(*SANK-tum sank-TOR-um*) A private secluded location;
literally, a holy place.

Knowing he was well-prepared,
    Familiar with the law,
The shrewd attorney pled his case,
    With obvious *sang-froid.*

(sahn-FRAW) Coolness, composure; literally,
cold blood.

Some playbills do not list "The Cast,"
    They think it's much more tony
To refer to all the actors as
    The *"Dramatis Personae."*

(DRAM-ah-tiss per-SOHN-ee) The cast of a stage play.

When a president, king, or CEO
    Is lacking expertise,
It helps to have a seasoned hand
    To serve as *éminence grise.*

(ay-mee-nahns GREEZ) A trusted advisor; the power
behind the throne; literally, gray eminence, a reference
to Cardinal Richelieu's gray-cloaked secretary.

The spicy gossip I have shared
    Is absolutely true,
But I'm sure you understand it's all
    Strictly *entre nous*.

(ON-tray NOO) Just between us.

The military puts recruits
    Through torment they abhor.
They think that mutual suffering
    Builds *esprit de corps*.

(ess-PREE de KOHR) Group spirit; fellowship.

In any proper sushi dish
    The fish is always raw.
To ask to have it slightly cooked
    Would be a gross *faux pas*.

(foh PAW) a breach of etiquette, a blunder;
literally, a false step.

Graffiti vandals victimize
   The neighborhoods they spray.
It almost makes you want to start
   A new *auto-da-fé*.

(*aw-toh dah FAY*) Punishment during the
Spanish Inquisition, usually by burning at the stake.

Her dress is quite revealing,
   She doesn't wear a bra,
Her swagger makes it obvious
   That she's a *fille de joie*.

(*fee de ZHWAH*) A prostitute; literally,
girl of joy.

You may not wolf your dinner down,
   Or slurp it like a pig,
But still your manners may appear
   Somewhat *infra dig*.

(*In-fruh DIG*) Undignified. Short for the Latin
phrase, *infra dignitatum*, beneath dignity.

A *non sequitur* in an argument
　　Adds nothing but confusion.
It occurs each time the premise
　　Doesn't lead to the conclusion.

(nohn SEK-wi-tur) An illogical argument.

Though children are often angelic and sweet,
　　There are times when they really torment us,
And you wish that somebody, just for a while,
　　Could serve *in loco parentis.*

(in LOH-KOH pah-REN-tiss) In place of a parent.

Despite the movie star's ignorance,
　　Her opinions are always deemed notable.
Because she is pretty and famous,
　　She is, *ipso facto,* quotable.

(IP-so FAK-to) By the fact itself; intrinsically.

He drinks too much and spends too much,
　　His account is overdrawn.
The problem is, he sees himself
　　As a *bon vivant.*

(*bohn vee-VAHN*) A person who lives the good life,
enjoying fine food, good drink, and luxurious living.

To one who's seen it all before
  The world is old, it's all a bore.
Events are stale, there's nothing new
  For one who's cursed with *déjà vu.*

(day-zhah VU) The feeling that an event being
encountered for the first time was experienced
previously; literally, already seen.

All your achievements,
  Whether modest or mighty,
Should be used to enhance
  Your *curriculum vitae.*

(kuh-RIK-you-lum VI-tee) A brief summary of one's
education and experience, usually for a job application;
literally, the course of one's life.

Our opportunities slip by
  So fast we hardly see 'em.
Deeds delayed are deeds forgot —
  Get busy, *carpe diem!*

(kar-pe DEE-em) Seize the day; enjoy the present.

The entry in a beauty contest
    Wanted to do well.
The natural look was "in," she'd heard,
    So she posed *au naturel.*

(o na-tyou-REL) Nude; literally, in the natural state.
It also refers to food served uncooked.

The singer did the best she could;
    The judges weren't impressed.
"You have a lovely voice" they said,
    (An obvious *beau geste*).

(bo zhest) A gracious, but usually insincere, comment.

Dishes baked in a casserole,
    Whether made from scratch or boughten,
Seem a bit more tantalizing
    When they're cooked *au gratin.*

(o grah-tin) With a covering of browned bread crumbs,
butter and grated cheese.

Sometimes when nations go to war
    The reason is a mystery.
The *casus belli* many times
    Is found in ancient history.

(KAH-sus BELL-eye) Cause of a war; reason for a quarrel.

Good politicians always strive
    To make their speeches flow,
And do their best to finish with
    A memorable *bon mot.*

(bohn MOH) An elegant expression or witty comment;
literally, a good word.

As symbols of their imperial power
    Kings display royal regalia,
Such as scepter and crown, a fine ermine gown,
    Or an ornate jeweled staff, *inter alia.*

(in-ter AY-lee-yuh) Among other things.

The club's dress code is flexible
    But one thing is for sure:
Though coat and tie are optional,
    Pants are *de regeuer.*

(deu ree-GUHR) Strictly required by custom.

I sometimes mispronounce a word,
    On that I must agree,
But "hypodemic nerdle"
    Was a weird *lapsus linguae.*

(LAP-sus ling-WEE) A slip of the tongue.

"I hate this cell," the prisoner said,
    "It's a lousy place to stay.
The bed and john are poorly placed —
    It's lacking in *feng shui!*"

(fung SHWAY) The Chinese art of situating furniture
and furnishings in accordance with spiritual
considerations such as yin and yang.

A statue of a movie star,
   In marble, bronze, or clay,
Would be a waste – a better choice
   Would be *papier-mâché.*

(pahp-YAY-ma-SHAY) Crushed paper mixed
with paste or glue; literally, chewed paper.

Your opponent's proofs may seem obscure,
   Disorganized and random.
He still might score a QED –
   Quod Erat Demonstrandum

(kwad er-aht dem-uhn-STRAN-dum) That which was
to have been demonstrated.

In writing a book about someone,
   His vices to portray,
It might be best to feature him
   In a *roman à clef.*

(roh-man ah KLAY) A novel in which real persons are
disguised as fictional characters; literally, novel with a key.

Said the geisha to the tourist,
   As she bowed in her kimono,
"I'd love to sing and dance for you,
   But I never perform *pro bono.*"

(proh BOH-noh) Anything done without charge.

A diet's not easy to follow,
    But they say you're what you eat.
So count your calories, watch your fats,
    It's time to start – *tout de suite!*

(toot SWEET) Immediately. (*Note:* the "de" is silent.)

Every snowflake, they say, is *sui generis,*
    A statement I strongly suspect.
They claim no two flakes in the world are the same–
    However, I doubt that they've checked.

(soo-ee JEN-air-iss) one-of-a-kind; unique.

Restaurants use some special terms
    In the prices that they quote;
A single figure for a meal
    Is known as *table d'hôte.*

(tah-bel DOHT) A meal, usually of several courses, for
which one pays a flat price irrespective of what one orders;
literally, host's table.

Teenagers silently ask themselves,
    "Just where do I belong?"
It's a period of uncertainty,
    A time of *Sturm und Drang*.

*(SHTOORM unt DRAHNG) storm and
struggle; emotional turmoil.*

Opinion polls have few hard facts
    On which you can rely,
For every pollster thinks he's found
    The true *vox populi*.

(vox POP-yool-eye) Voice of the people;
popular sentiment.

Though outnumbered and battered and bruised
    The regiment stayed the course.
The battle they won against all odds
    Was a marvelous *tour de force*.

(toor de FORSS) A feat of exceptional strength
or skill; an outstanding achievement.

You get more than shampoos
    In the beauty salon —
An update on gossip
    Is the *sine qua non.*

(SEE-neh kwah NON) Essential element.

Women and men have similar roles
    With similar needs and wants.
But although the gap is narrowing,
    Vive la différence!

(VEEV la dee-fay-ROHNS) Long live the difference.

For helping clients break the law
    The lawyer was disbarred.
He said, "I'm not a criminal –
    I'm merely *avant-garde.*"

(ah-vanht-GAHRD) Innovative, ahead of the times;
literally, advance guard.

When the embassy's ambassador
   Is neither here nor there,
All decisions must be made
   By the *chargé d'affaires.*

(shar-ZHAY dah-FAIR) The person in charge of a diplomatic
mission in the absence of the ambassador or minister.

The thoughtless dude who fills a room
   With fumes of a cigar
Is a most obnoxious, odious,
   And odorous *bête noir.*

(bet NWAHR) Something or someone who is
particularly disliked; literally, black beast.

If movie actors botch their lines
   And flub the words they say,
No problem – advertise it as
   Cinéma vérité.

(sin-ee-mah VAIR-ee-TAY) Realistic film-making.

Tatooists are constantly looking for skin
    On which they can do what they do.
They see a bare arm as a *tabula rasa,*
    A site for another tattoo.

(TAH-boo-lah RAH-zah) A clean slate, anything existing
in its pristine condition; literally, scraped tablet.

If, when you weigh the pros and cons,
    It all comes out a draw,
It doesn't matter which you choose,
    Because *comme ci, comme ça.*

(kom SEE kom SAH) Like this, like that; a tossup.

Southern gentry and Southern belles
    Behaved with great propriety.
Social conventions were always observed
    In *ante bellum* society.

(AN-tee BELL-um) Before the war. Usually referring
to the American Civil war of 1861-1865.

He met her at a local bar,
    A sexy chick, a gem.
She and his wallet soon disappeared –
    Cherchez la femme!

(sher-shay la fem) Search for the woman. (Usually
refers to the motive behind a crime, or the clue to
solving a mystery.)

Of all the torments on a plane,
   I think the most appalling
Is sitting near an *enfant terrible*
   Who simply won't stop squalling.

(on-fon teh-REE-bluh) An incorrigible child, a brat.

No amount of planning makes you
   Totally secure.
There's no way to protect yourself
   Against a *force majeure*.

(forss mah-JUHR) An irresistible force, or an event
over which one has no control; literally, superior force.

Instead of pleading guilty
   For conduct that's unlawful,
To plead *nolo contendere*
   Does not sound quite so awful.

(NOH-loh con-TEN-deh-reh) A plea made by a
defendant that is virtually, but not technically,
an admission of guilt.

The toy store had a thousand things
    To fill a small boy's wants,
But the Star Wars blaster ray gun
    Was the *pièce de résistance.*

(PYESS de ray-zee-STAHNS) The most desirable
item in a collection.

When Frenchmen speak of *escargot,*
    Snails are what they mean.
What we consider garden pests
    In France are *haute cuisine.*

(es-kar-GO) Snail.
(oht kwee-ZEEN) Gourmet cooking.

A small one-room apartment
    With just a bed and chair
Is not so nice, but could suffice
    As a *pied-à-terre.*

(pee-ED ah TAIR) A small apartment for
temporary or occasional use; literally,
foot on the ground.

You can't help but pity
    The Sorcerer's Apprentice –
He's someone who's obviously
    Non compos mentis.

(non com-pos MEN-tiss) Mentally unstable.

In public demonstrations
    The leaders must ensure
That a seeming friend is not, in fact,
    An *agent provocateur.*

(a-ZHAN pro-vok-a-TUR) A person associating with
suspected individuals or groups to incite them to commit
acts that would make them liable to punishment.

He was a dapper modern man,
    His style he loved to flaunt.
The clothes he wore, the oaths he swore,
    Were always *au courant.*

(oh coo RAHN) up-to-date, current, well-informed.

Two lovers met with open arms
    Beneath the mistletoe.
He kissed her first, then she kissed him —
    A case of *quid pro quo.*

(kwid pro kwoh) Something given or taken in
return for something else.

A football player may gain fame
　　For a pass he caught one Sunday.
By Saturday his name's forgot –
　　Sic transit gloria mundi.

(Sik TRANS-it GLO-ree-uh MUN-dee) Thus
passes away the glory of the world.

Although his client was accused
　　Of conduct gross and racy,
The lawyer knew the evidence
　　Was only *prima facie.*

(PREE-ma FAY-shee) At first glance, not yet proven.

If, when those around you
　　Are floundering in despair,
You always act with poise and tact
　　You're blessed with *savoir-faire.*

(sav-wahr-FAIR) Sophistication; literally, to
know how to act.

We are all created equal,
  The meaning of which varies:
Though we're all considered equal,
  Some are *primus inter pares*.

(PREE-mus in-ter PAIR-eez) First among equals.

To simply write RSVP
  Is the customary way.
It's easier than writing out
  Répondez s'il vous plaît.

(ray-POHN-day seel voo PLAY) Please reply;
literally, respond if it pleases you.

A Marine's blushing bride
  Need never be jealous,
He'll always be true to her –
  Semper fidelis.

(sem-pehr fee-DAY-lis) Always faithful;
the motto of the U.S. Marine Corps.

The argument *ad hominem*
   Is something people use
When logic, facts and reason
   Don't support their views.

(ad HAWM-in-em) Argument attacking the
individual instead of analyzing relevant issues.

When faced with an impending threat
   Most folks fight or flee.
Others shrug and sit it out,
   Insisting, *"C'est la vie."*

(say la VEE) That's life.

Suppose you work and scheme and plot
   To be a billionaire.
Would you then guess that your success
   Is likely? *Au contraire!*

(oh kon-TRAIR) On the contrary.

Although a simple table wine
    Is perfectly okay,
You could spend just a trifle more
    And get a *vin de pays*.

(van duh PAY) In the French wine-ranking system, this
is a step above table wine (*vin ordinaire*), with grapes
from a specific location; literally, wine of the country.

I shared a secret with some friends,
    I thought it would delight 'em.
They promptly shared it with *their* friends,
    And so *ad infinitum*.

(ad in-fi-NYE-tum) To infinity; forever.

Though politicians always claim
    Their actions are transparent,
The deals they make *sub rosa*
    Are often not apparent.

(sub RO-sah) In secret; literally, "under the rose,"
the rose being the symbol of secrecy in certain
ancient societies.

To confirm the understandings
    That we have reached thus far,
Perhaps it would be prudent
    To prepare an *aide-memoire*.

(ayd mem-WAHR) A written summary of
decisions reached during negotiations; literally
memory aid.

When you've double-crossed your friends,
    When you've acted like a crook,
Just saying "*Mea culpa*"
    Doesn't get you off the hook.

(MAY-ah KUL-pah) I am guilty; it is my fault.

When the husband criticized his wife
    For purchasing a launch,
She said, "Well, after all, my dear,
    Your gift card said *carte blanche.*"

(kart BLANSH) Complete authority to act as one
wishes; literally, white card.

A political opponent won't
   Require extensive proof,
He'll make a *cause célèbre*
   From just a minor goof.

(kohz say-LEH-bre) A highly controversial
matter that gains broad public attention; literally,
famous case.

Fashion models never smile,
   They're solemn and demure.
But when they're downright sullen
   They're modeling *haute couture.*

(oht koo-TOUR) High fashion dress design.

The role of the Vice President
   Is rather vague, although
He chairs the Senate's talkathons
   Ex officio.

(ex oh-FISH-ee-oh) By virtue of the office.

A style that shook the world of art
   Many years ago,
With flowing curves and foliate forms,
   Was known as *art nouveau.*

(ahrt noo-VOH) A style of decorative art popular in
the late 19th and early 20th centuries, featuring sinuous
lines and intricate designs; literally, new art.

Though not a party in the trial,
    A person may apply
To submit opinions to the court
    As *amicus curiae*.

(ah-MEE-kus KUR-ee-eye) A party permitted to offer
advice or information to the court during a proceeding.

A slice of chicken, a slice of ham,
    A slice of cheese (for glue);
Sauté them all together,
    The result is *cordon bleu*.

(kor-dohn BLOO) Thin slices, as described;
literally, blue ribbon. The term also refers to
the award given a master chef.

It takes a skillful diplomat
    To mediate a brawl,
But with patience you can sometimes reach
    An *entente cordiale*.

(awn-tawnt kor-dee-AWL) A friendly agreement.

A rule to follow if you'd write
    A good detective story:
The killer's named in the *dénouement*,
    Never *a priori*.

(day-noo-MAHN) At the end of a novel, the
untangling of a plot; literally, unraveling.
(aw pree-OH-ree) Beforehand.

Some kings and queens and presidents
    Prolong their last hurrah.
There seems no way to nudge them out
    Short of a *coup d'état*.

(koo day-TAH) A sudden takeover of a government
by rebel forces; literally, stroke of state.

Your existence isn't something
    That you can just presume.
The proof is when you tell yourself,
    Cogito, ergo sum.

(KOG-ee-toh ER-go SUM) I think, therefore I am.
(The foundation of the philosophy of Descartes.)

The boxer's legs were wobbly,
   He sensed a coming loss.
His opponent scored an uppercut,
   Which was the *coup de grâce.*

(*koo de GRAHSS*) A final blow. Originally it meant the
"gracious" act of killing a mortally wounded combatant
to end his suffering.

When a twist of fate has caused you
   All the pain you can endure,
It's only human nature
   To emit a *cri de coeur.*

(*kree de KUHR*) Cry from the heart; a
heartfelt plea.

When the boss puts his foot down
   I'm sure you'll agree
That the "fate" of his edict
   Is a *fait accompli.*

(*FAY-tuh KAHM-PLEE*) An accomplished fact.

When served in ample quantity
  In goblet, cup or glass,
Liquor oft uncovers truth:
  In vino veritas.

(in VEE-no VER-ee-tass) In wine there is truth.

In a fashionable restaurant,
  Any diner will agree,
You'll get much better service
  If you tip the *maitre d'.*

(MET-ruh DEE) The chief headwaiter or manager
of a restaurant or hotel. Short for *maître d'hôtel.*

The bandit's car was filled with loot,
  Police cars sped in hot pursuit.
He turned, to throw the cops off track—
  Alas, it was a *cul-de-sac.*

(kul-de-sak) A street closed at one end; literally,
bottom of a bag.

Where there's a will there is a way,
  And that's the fatal flaw
In the self-defeating attitude of
  Que sera, sera.

(kay ser-ah ser-ah) What will be, will be.

A beach bathed in moonlight,
  Some friends, a guitar,
The glow of a campfire –
  It's *sehr wünderbar.*

(zer VOON-der bahr) Very wonderful.

The bride enjoys the social swirl
  Before the nuptial hour.
If the wedding is *al fresco*, though,
  She may get one more shower!

(al fres-ko) Out of doors.

The oriental martial arts
  Are useful skills to know:
Karate, judo or *kung fu,*
  Or Olympic *taekwando.*

*(kuh-RAW-tee, JOO-do, kung FOO, teye-kwan-DO) The
marital arts are intended for defense, exercise, and spiritual
development. Karate is Okinawan, judo Japanese, kung fu
Chinese, and taekwando Korean.*

A certain young lady came out of her room
   In a dress that was shockingly scanty.
Her mother said, "Darling, put on some clothes,
   And return to the *status quo ante*."

(*stay-tus quo AN-tee*) The previous condition.

Vers libre can be lyrical,
   Evocative, sublime.
Still, you cannot help but wonder:
   Is there something wrong with rhyme?

(*vair LEE-bru*) Free verse; poetry lacking meter,
rhyme, or structure.

Ordering that featured dinner
   May not be so smart:
You'd save both cash and calories
   If you ordered *á la carte*.

(*a lah KAHRT*) According to the menu, with
each item priced separately.

When someone thrives in his career,
  And attains the peak thereof,
Friends will say "Congrats!" "Bravo!"
  Or maybe *"Mazel tov!"*

(MAH-zel tahv) Congratulations! Also, good luck!

When badgered by the IRS
  His profits to declare,
The tycoon said, "This violates
  The code of *laissez-faire.*"

(les-ay FEHR) Opposition to government regulation
of commerce; literally, allow to act.

A type of eye-wear once in vogue,
  But seldom seen today,
Was thought to add a touch of class;
  They called it a *pince-nez.*

(pans-NAY) Eyeglasses popular during the 19th and early 20th
centuries, clamped on the bridge of the nose, often attached to
a cord or chain; literally, pinch nose.

If that favorite dish you're cooking
　　Isn't quite what it should be,
Don't offer explanations,
　　Just say, *"Bon appétit!"*

(bon ah-pay-TEE) Enjoy your meal.

If there's someone you have harmed
　　Resolve it now, don't wait.
Apologies made *in extremis*
　　Come a bit too late.

(in eks-TRAY-miss) At the point of death.

If one event precedes another,
　　It doesn't prove a link.
But *post hoc ergo propter hoc*
　　Is how some people think.

(post hok air-go PROP-ter hok) The illogical
belief that if one event precedes another it must
have caused the other. Often referred to as the
post hoc fallacy.

If you'll just take me as I am
   I'll take you as you are.
But if you want to make me over,
   Darling, *au revoir.*

(oh re-VWAHR) Goodbye.

Some folks like to grill their meat
   On a charcoal barbecue.
Others claim it's more delicious
   Cooked and served *au jus.*

(oh ZHU) Meat roasted and served in its natural
juices or gravy.

The indispensable technique
   A leader has to know
Is how to foster in his flock
   The spirit of *gung ho.*

(gung HOH) Enthusiastic attitude; from a
Chinese term meaning "work together."

The term, "the lower middle class"
   Is one we sometimes see.
But snobs prefer to use the phrase,
   The *petite bourgeoisie.*

(*peu-teet boor-zhwah-ZEE*) The least affluent middle
class: shopkeepers, artisans, clerical workers, etc.

My broker knows the market well,
   He counsels me a lot.
He tells me, *ex post facto,*
   Which stocks I should have bought.

(*ex post FAK-toh*) Applying to things that are in the past.

The ruby is glamorous, the emerald dazzling,
   Each is a beautiful gem,
And a gift of a pearl will impress any girl,
   But a diamond's the *crème de la crème.*

(*KREM de la KREM*) The very best; literally,
cream of the cream.

Layer on layer of different liqueurs,
  Arranged in a singular way,
Are the ultimate test of the bartender's art:
  They call it a *pousse-café*.

(poos kah-FAY) A drink consisting of liqueurs of various
densities, poured to form multicolored layers, usually served
after coffee; literally, push coffee.

While personal opinions
  Are open to dispute,
Ex cathedra proclamations
  Are harder to refute.

(ex kah-THEE-drah) "Official" pronouncements
made in the exercise of one's office or position.

You'll do it when you "find the time."
  Well, how about today?
Postponed tasks grow more unpleasant,
  Tempus fugit – don't delay!

(TEM-pus FYOO-jit) Time flies.

Selling guns and tanks and armor
    Has made many a millionaire.
The secret of their opulence?
    It's simple: *C'est la guerre!*

(*say lah GAIR*) It's the war. (Usually an expression
of resignation.)

The president held his predecessors
    In very low esteem;
He called them all, collectively,
    The *ancien régime.*

(*ahn-see-ahn ray-ZHEEM*) A political system that
no longer exists, originally referring to France prior
to the revolution of 1789.

Whenever you're insulted
    Your ego gets a boost
If without hesitation
    You respond with a *mot juste.*

(*moh JOOST*) The right word; a perfect expression.

Words like "cool" mean different things
    To different generations.
We need a *lingua franca*
    To enhance communications.

(LING-gwah FRAHN-kah) A language, or mixture
of languages, used by people who speak different
first languages.

Though traditionally the man is boss,
    Remaining so for life,
The *de facto* head of household
    Is frequently the wife.

(dee FAK-toh) Existing in reality, though not so designated.

To whet the diners' appetite
    For a meal you plan to serve
You'll often find it helpful
    To start with an *hors d'oeuvre*.

(or DEU-vre) An appetizer served before
the meal; literally, outside the work.

An injured athlete who plays through the pain,
    Is reluctant to withdraw,
But sometimes it's best for him and the team
    If he's classified *hors de combat.*

(ohr deu kom-BAH) Out of action; disabled; literally,
out of the fight.

The playboy said, describing his date,
    "She's a sweetheart, a dreamboat, a gem.
She's one in a million, the girl I adore,
    She's the love of my life (*pro tem*)."

(pro TEM) Temporarily. Short for *pro tempore.*

If you have an ailment, serious or slight,
    My herbalist knows how to fix it.
He has herbs that cure cancer, lumbago or flu.
    You need proof? Well, it's just *ipse dixit.*

(IP-see DIX-it) He himself said it; an assertion not
backed up by evidence.

Hitler, Stalin and Saddam Hussein
    Were reviled by those who had known 'em,
But let's just call them "world-famous leaders,"
    Because *de mortuis nil nisi bonum.*

(day MOR-too-ees nil nee-see BOH-num) Speak
nothing but good of the deceased,

Our amateur rock band made so much noise
    The neighbors could no longer stand us.
They said, "Tone it down or we call the police,"
    Now we practice *mutatis mutandis.*

(moo-TAH-tiss moo-TAND-diss) Necessary changes having
been made.

Though you were the first to suggest the idea,
    Someone else got all of the credit.
But you can't go through life regretting the past,
    Lo pasado, pasado. Forget it!

(loh pah-SAH-doh pah-SAH-doh) The past is past.

A certain young man was a victim of hiccups,
    His tummy incessantly jerked.
In sheer desperation he stood on his head
    And – *mirabile dictu* – it worked!

(*mee-RAH-bee-leh DIK-too*) Marvelous to say;
wonderful to relate.

When speaking to his boss he uses
    Words that fawn and flatter.
His *sotto voce* comments, though,
    Are quite a different matter.

(SOHT-oh VOH-cheh) Very quiet speech; whispered.

Politicians feuding by press release
    Rarely land a blow.
A *mano a mano* confrontation
    Makes for a better show.

(MAH-noh ah MAH-noh) A direct face-to-face
confrontation; literally, hand-to-hand.

In countries where they speak Spanish,
    In virtually every locale
You'll find that the principal highway
    Is called *El Camino Real.*

(el kah-MEE-noh ray-AL) The main road;
literally, the royal highway.

Running fast and catching prey,
  Is a sweet life for the cheetah.
One big feast, one long nap,
  That's *la dolce vita*.

(lah DOHL-chay VEE-tah) The sweet life.

Since farewell comments should observe
  The local protocol,
In southern Mexico should you say,
  "*Hasta la vista*, y'all"?

(HAH-stah lah VEE-stah) Until we meet;
see you later.

Good surgeons always keep in mind
  The burden that they carry,
Bound by the Hippocratic oath:
  Primum non nocere.

(PREE-mum non noh-KAIR-ee) First, do no harm.

Sometimes problems causing
  Acrimonious debate
Could be resolved if those involved
  Just had a *tête-a-tête*.

(TAYT-a-TAYT) A private discussion between
two people.

Negotiate, negotiate,
  When purchasing antiques.
Remember that the asking price
  Is never a *prix fixe*.

(pree FEEX) A fixed price for whatever is on a menu,
in contrast to *a la carte*.

The hero of the play looked bad,
  He seemed a callous crook.
It would take *deus ex machina*
  To get him off the hook.

(DAY-us ex MAH-kee-nah) An improbable event or
device to solve a difficult problem in a drama;
literally, "god from the machine." In ancient
Greek and Roman drama a god was lowered by a
crane onto the stage to resolve a difficulty in the plot.

Not only did they trim our hair,
    But barbers used to shave us.
Today, a man who gets a shave
    Is quite a *rara avis*.

(RAH-rah AY-viss) An unusual person; anything
not commonly encountered; literally, rare bird.

When his girl friend lamented
    She thought herself plain,
Her lover assured her
    "Bei mir bist du shoen."

(by meer bist doo shayn) To me, you are
beautiful.

When unforeseen disaster hits,
    No matter who's at fault,
A term conveying shock and pain
    Is simply, *"Oy, gevald!"*

(oy gevawlt) A Yiddish cry of anguish,
suffering, or frustration.

In judging a friend's poetry,
    If you detect a flaw,
Just say, "Your verse is interesting,
    It has… *je ne sais quoi.*"

(*je ne say KWAH*) An elusive, indefinable quality;

A big meal chalks up calories,
    Pie *a la mode* adds more,
Because of that, your best dessert
    May be a *petit four.*

(*pet-ee FOR*) A bite-sized pastry; literally,
little oven.

Some critics like to lavish praise,
    Some take a different tack.
One trend-setter's *objet d'art*
    Is another's *bric-a-brac.*

(*ob-zhay DAWR*) Works of art, usually small objects.
(*brik-a-brak*) Miscellaneous small articles of little value.

When a person's speech is rambling,
    Ambiguous and flighty,
Sometimes it isn't ignorance –
    Just too much *aqua vitae*.

(ack-wah VI-tee) Strong distilled alcohol, such as
brandy or whiskey; literally, water of life.

If the seller seems quite desperate
    To get you to decide,
You cannot help but wonder
    If the offer's *bona fide*.

(BOHN-a-fyd) Legitimate; made in good faith.

A speeding car hit an ice cream truck
    On a little country road.
The resulting scene might be described
    As wreckage *à la mode*.

(Ah lah MOHD) In the United States the term usually
refers to a dessert served with ice cream. The literal
meaning is "fashionable."

She may seem a platonic friend,
    A confidant, a pal,
But be on guard – she may turn out
    To be a *femme fatale.*

(fam feh-TAHL) A seductive woman who leads
men into disastrous intrigues or situations.

When a politician claims to speak
    Without a trace of malice,
Such mealy-mouthed assurances
    I take *cum grano salis.*

(kum GRANE-o SAL-iss) With a grain of salt.

Some things in my life, I fear,
    Have been a bit bizarre.
I think I'll use a *nom de plume*
    When writing my memoir.

(nom de PLOOM) A name used to conceal
the writer's identity; literally, pen name.

A poet's heart convinces him
    His efforts are worthwhile.
His *raison d'être* is to share
    An insight ... or a smile.

(ray-zohn DET-ruh) Justification for existence;
literally, reason to be.

About the Author

A former journalist, lobbyist, lecturer, and business consultant, Ed Bliss is author of *Getting Things Done, Are Your Employees Stealing You Blind?*, *Doing it Now,* and *A Friendly Discussion,* Now retired, he lives in Lompoc, California.

Index

reductio ad absurdum (L) 7
repondez si'l vous plait (F) 30
roman à clef (F) 17

sanctum sanctorum (L) 7
sang froid (F) 8
sans souci (F) 1
savoir-faire (F) 29
sehr vunderbar (G) 40
semper fidelis (L) 30
sic gloria transit mundi (L) 29
sine qua non (L) 21
sotto voce (It) 53
status quo ante (L) 42
Sturm und Drang (G) 20
sub rosa (L) 32
sui generis (L) 19
summa cum laude (L) 6

table d'hote (F) 19
tabula rasa (L) 23
taekwondo (K) 41
tempus fugit (L) 47

tête-à-tête (F) 55
tour de force (F) 20
tout de suite (F) 19
tout le monde (F) 5

vers libre (F) 42
vin de pays (F) 32
vive la difference (F) 21
vox populi (L) 20

C Chinese
F French
G German
Gr Greek
I Italian
J Japanese
K Korean
L Latin
P Portugese
S Spanish
Y Yiddish

65